BACKYARD SCIENTIST

By Jane Hoffman

ILLUSTRATED by LANNY OSTROFF

The award winning Backyard Scientist hands-on series includes:

Backyard Scientist, Series One gives children ages 4 to 12 more fun and fascinating ways to explore chemistry and physics. *Backyard Scientist, Series Two* will astonish the 9- to 14-year-old with thrilling experiments in chemistry and physics. *Backyard Scientist, Series Three* for 4- to 12-year-olds shifts gears with experiments in entomology, biology and physiology. *Backyard Scientist, Series Four* is a great family book containing exciting and stimulating experiments for scientists of all ages. Nine- to 14-year-old students will especially like this collection of experiments. Its focus is on chemistry and physics. *Exploring Earthworms With Me*, an American Booksellers Association PICK OF THE LIST, is written for the 4- to 12-year-old who wants to learn everything about these interesting and beneficial creatures with an exciting array of hands-on projects.

These books are excellent for independent study or classroom/group activity.

Each title will thrill and delight your young scientist. Great ideas for science fair projects.

The Original Backyard Scientist

Summer 1987
Published by Backyard Scientist/Jane Hoffman
P.O. Box 16966
Irvine, CA 92623
©1987 (revised edition) by Backyard Scientist/Jane Hoffman

0-9618663-1-4

TABLE OF CONTENTS

THE REVIEWS ARE IN ON BACKYARD SCIENTIST
WHAT EDUCATORS AND PARENTS ARE SAYING ABOUT THE BACKYARD SCIENTIST

"For the easiest and most enjoyable approach to science experiments, I recommend (The Backyard Scientist) by Jane Hoffman."

-- Mary Pride
The Teaching Home

"Her goal (is) to see the public school system adopt an ongoing, daily, hands-on science curriculum. No one can say that Jane Hoffman isn't doing her part to try to achieve this aim."

-- Nita Kurmins Gilson
The Christian Science Monitor

("Hoffman's) own curiosity and energy are a large part of the appeal of The Backyard Scientist. 'I believe that science makes a difference in the way a child learns.'"

--The Chicago Tribune

"Anyone who can read, or get an assistant to read, can have fun building the experiments described in The Backyard Scientist series and then have even more fun using (Hoffman's) experiments to explore science."

-- Paul Doherty, Ph.D.
Physicist/Teacher

"What makes these experiments special is their hands-on nature. A firm believer that science makes a difference in how a child learns, Hoffman encourages kids to think for themselves, to ask questions and to observe the world around them."

-- Science Books and Films

"All of the experiments have been pre-tested extensively with groups of children."

-- Curriculum Product News Magazine

"I believe that you have many of the answers to our problems with science education in the early grades."

~ Mary Kohleman
National Science Foundation
Washington, DC

"There are a lot of good reasons why you should order the books, but if you need another one, just remember you're doing it for a worthy cause--your students."

--Teaching K-8 Magazine

"Popcorn, ice cubes and string are among the materials used in her experiments...most of which the children conduct themselves. But the main ingredient is the enthusiasm that Jane generates in the fledgling scientists!."

-- Women's Day Magazine

"...(Backyard Scientist series) is the best 'hands-on' experience a young reader can help him or herself to. Original and highly recommended for schools and home-teaching."

-- Children's Bookwatch

"As a teacher, I truly appreciated your book. It was well organized and easy to follow. The experience with a variety of scientific concepts has sparked further interest in several areas with many of the

students. They have asked for more!"*

-- Amy Korenack
Resource Teacher

"She makes science come alive."

-- Orange Coast Daily Pilot

"Backyard Scientest teaches children the art of thinking."

-- Anaheim Bulletin

"My mom is a teacher and thinks these books are the greatest."

-- Ryan, Age 5

"I loved the 'Backyard Scientist Series.' I like things I hadn't thought of doing by myself."

-- Chris, Age 7

"I loved the 'Backyard Scientist' books. They are so great." -

- Thomas Age 8-1/2

"I tried your experiments with my students and they went wild with excitement."

-- First Grade Teacher, Illinois

"I really appreciate the clear instructions, simple to get household supplies, and the complete and easy to understand explanations. Thanks for these wonderful books."

-- Mrs. Getz, Home Schooling Mom

In between getting up in the morning, taking my son to school, teaching science classes for thousands of kids all over Orange County, California, cleaning the house (sometimes), doing the wash, going to the market, and cooking (one does have to eat), driving my son to basketball practice and watching all his games (he is in two leagues), and coping with my husband who wonders why I "never have any time and what I do all day anyhow?", I have managed to write this, my first science book, in my spare time.

Kids are truly wonderful people and so I dedicate this, my first book, to my son Jason, his friends, and all the kids who have been in my classes.

Jane Hoffman

FOREWORD

The single most influential developmental psychologist in the world today is Jean Piaget. His many contributions on the development of human intelligence have provided psychologists, educators, and parents with significant insights into children's behavior and the way in which they learn and process information. Piaget has helped us to understand how children perceive their world at different ages as well as why they are asking questions and interpreting information the way that they do. Piaget found that the young child learns best about how the world around him works by touching, smelling, pouring, testing, experimenting, and playing. However, while the child is doing this discovery about his world he is also organizing his new experiences by differentiation, integration, and categorization. As he grows and matures his mind becomes increasingly alert and curious causing him to question and further explore and experiment until he finds answers that satisfy him or cause him to begin a new and more complex level of activity and exploration. It is through this process of maturation, exploration, and discovery that the child's mind grows and develops into more complex stages of cognition.

The overriding implication of Piaget's theory of cognitive development for educators and parents is that in order for the child to learn in a deliberate and lasting manner he should be actively involved in discovering new experiences because during the process of discovery and experimentation the child is exploring with his senses, discovering relations by direct experience, manipulating, transforming, categorizing, and combining materials. He is also describing and expressing his feelings and ideas, noticing differences, similarities, and transformations. By doing these kinds of activities the child is developing the fundamental concepts that are essential for future learning and intellectual growth.

The study of science provides the child with all the necessary ingredients needed for active learning and cognitive growth. Therefore, it is one of the best avenues through which the child can learn about the world around him. As an example, through scientific experimentation the child learns how to represent experiences and ideas, how to use language effectively, and how to develop logical reasoning skills. We can as educators and parents help the child discover constancies among his changing world as well as help him establish intellectual growth and security by providing him with relevant forms of activity such scientific experimentation provides. Mental growth is dynamic, and by encouraging discovery, questioning experimentation, and exploration in science, intellectual development is enhanced.

Marie Toni Mulherin, Ed. D.
February 24, 1983

Welcome to your first class of the "Backyard Scientist." I am going to turn you all into young scientists. Do you like to explore? Be a private detective? Solve problems? Figure things out for yourselves? See exciting things happen? Investigate things around you? Do you like daring adventures? Wonder why things happen? If your answer is "yes" to any of these questions, then you are going to have fun being a "Backyard Scientist." When we finish the series of experiments in this book, you may send me your name and address and a stamped self-addressed envelope, telling me you have com-pleted all the experiments in the book and what you thought of them, and which ones were your favorites. I will send back to you an official "Backyard Scientist" Certificate certifying that you are a "Backyard Scientist." Your name will be in the official "Backyard Scientist Club."

Come, let us enter into the world of the "Backyard Scientist." Let's all put on our thinking caps and think science, because once you start an experiment, you become a scientist exploring just like scientists do in laboratories. Imagine wherever you are working is your laboratory, and you are ready to start the experiment.

As a Backyard Scientist working in your laboratories there are some very important guide lines you must follow:

1. **ALWAYS** work with an adult.
2. **NEVER,** never, taste anything you are experimenting with except when instructed to do so in the experiment.
3. **ALWAYS** follow the Backyard Scientist directions in the experiment
4. **ALWAYS** wash your hands with soap and warm water after you finish experimenting.
5. **BE A PATIENT** scientist. Some experiments take longer than others before results can be observed.
6. If you have any questions about any of the experiments, write me, Jane Hoffman, The Backyard Scientist, P.O. Box 16966, Irvine, CA 92623.

You are ready to start experimenting. Have fun. When you complete all of the experiments be sure to read how to get your Backyard Scientist Certificate and how to join the Backyard Scientist Club. Details are at the back of the book.

Happy Experimenting,

Jane Hoffman

Your Friend,
Jane Hoffman
The Backyard Scientist

The Case of the Disappearing Life Savers

Your scientific mission for this experiment is to use your thinking powers and observation skills to explore and gather all the evidence you can. The secret code words are solutions, dissolving, range, average, computed, minimum, maximum, visible, invisible, surface area, and molecule. In this mission you will need some friends to assist you in the investigation. Good luck. This will now self-destruct in 1 minute. Gather these clues; you will need them to solve the following science cases.

Clues
"Life Savers"—different colors
Paper and pencil
Clock or watch
2 small (2 oz. to 5 oz.) plastic cups, preferably one that you see through. If you do not have plastic cups, paper cups will do just fine.
Toothpicks
Water—cold from tap

Gather these clues for case #1
"Life Savers"—different colors
Paper and pencil
Clock or watch

Begin your investigation
Everyone get ready to put a "Life Saver" in your mouth, and to write down the time it goes into your mouth on the piece of paper everyone has. Someone say, "1, 2, 3, go," and write down the time that the "Life Saver" went into your mouths. Now, everyone is allowed to suck on the "Life Saver," and not bite into it. Keep watching the clock or watch and

as soon as the "Life Saver" is dissolved in your mouth, write down that time on the piece of paper. After you have all dissolved the "Life Savers" in your mouths, see who was first, second, third and so on. Compare with each other to find the average time for dissolving the "Life Savers." What made the "Life Saver" disappear in your mouths? What was the range for dissolving the "Life Saver"?

Solution to case #1

The saliva (moisture or wetness) and sucking motion (pressure) in your mouths made the "Life Savers" disappear. The average time for dissolving the "Life Savers" in your mouths can be computed by adding up the total time of all who did the experiment and dividing by the number of children who were involved in the experiment. To find the range, you take the minimum to the maximum times. You gather these times after you have computed the average time. Example: Range — it took 1-7 minutes.

Gather these clues for case #2

"Life Savers" — use red, green or orange colored ones
Paper and pencil
Clock or watch
1 small glass — 2 oz. to 5 oz. size
Water — cold from tap (enough to fill up the glass)

Begin your investigation

Take a "Life Saver" and put it into the glass of water. Now mark down on a piece of paper the time you put the "Life Saver" into the water. Observe the "Life Saver" in the water. What happened after 5 minutes? What is the "Life Saver" doing in the cup? Keep watching the "Life Saver" until it is completely dissolved in the water. Mark down the time on your piece of paper when the "Life Saver" completely dissolved. What was happening to the "Life Saver" as it was dissolving in the cup of water? Is the "Life Saver" a solid object? Why do you think that? Is the water a liquid? Why? What part of the human body compares with a glass? What affects the rate of dissolving?

Solution to case #2

The "Life Saver" is dissolving slowly in the cup of water. As the "Life Saver" dissolved, you were observing these things happen:

1. The "Life Saver" is shrinking or getting smaller.

2. The water is taking on the color of the "Life Saver."

3. The "Life Saver" is taking on a new shape.

The "Life Saver" is a solid object, because it doesn't change shape easily; another solid can't be passed through it easily and a solid object is usually visible.

The water is a liquid; liquids can change shape easily, may be visible or invisible, and objects can pass through them easily.

Our mouths compare with a glass. Temperature, motion and surface area all have an effect on the rate of something dissolving.

Gather these clues for case #3
"Life Savers" — use red, green or orange colored ones
Paper and pencil
Clock or watch
1 small glass — 2 oz. to 5 oz.
Water — cold from tap (enough to fill the small glass
Toothpick

Begin your investigation

Place the "Life Saver" into the glass of water. Mark down on the piece of paper the time you put the "Life Saver" in the water. Now pick up the toothpick and start to stir the water and keep stirring until the "Life Saver" is completely dissolved in the water. Then write down the time on the piece of paper that the "Life Saver" dissolved into the water. Did the "Life Saver" dissolve faster when stirring it with the toothpick, than it did in case #1? What compares to water in the human body?

Solution to case #3

Yes, the "Life Saver" dissolved faster stirring it with the toothpick than when not stirring it. Motion affects the rate of dissolving. You are moving the liquid with the toothpick. More water molecules are moving past the "Life Saver." The saliva in our mouths can be compared to the water in the experiment. They both serve the same purpose in dissolving the "Life Savers."

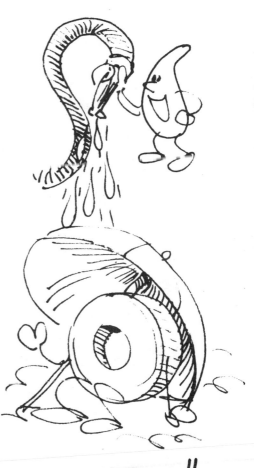

The Case of the Mysterious Gas

Your scientific mission for this experiment is to use your thinking powers and observation skills to explore and gather all the evidence you can. The secret code words are gas, atoms, expand, reaction, molecule, pressure, the chemical symbols H_2O and CO_2, and chemical change. Good luck. This will now self–destruct in 1 minute. Gather these clues; you will need them to solve the following science cases.

Clues

Baking soda
White distilled vinegar
Balloons — with the neck of the balloon cut off
Ziploc storage bags — quart size
Glass bottle with a small mouth (8 oz. size is good)
Measuring cup and spoon

Cork — to fit tightly into the small bottle (make sure there are no holes in it)
Paper cups — 3 oz. size
Funnel — any small plastic or metal funnel will do

Gather these clues for case #1

2 paper cups — 3 oz. size
Baking Soda — 1 heaping tbsp.
Vinegar - (white distilled) 1/4 cup

Begin your investigation

Take 2 paper cups. In one cup place 1 tbsp. baking soda and in the other cup place 1/4 cup of vinegar. Now look at the cup with the baking soda in it. Do you see anything happening to it or is it just lying in the cup? Smell the baking soda. Do you smell anything? Now smell the vinegar. Do you smell anything? What do you think will happen if we mix the two together? Let's try it and see.

Carefully pick up the cup with the vinegar in it and pour it slowly into the cup with the baking soda in it. Now watch closely. Don't take your eyes off it for a second. What is happening? When the vinegar and baking soda were mixed together, a gas was released. Do you know the name of the gas? Where did the gas go? What observations did you notice when the baking soda and vinegar were mixed together? Do you know some of the ways carbon dioxide is useful to people?

Solution to case #1

The mixing of the vinegar with the baking soda caused a bubbling and fizzing effect. When we poured the vinegar into the baking soda, a chemical change took place and the gas, carbon dioxide, was released. Scientists don't use the words carbon dioxide. They have shortened it and use the chemical symbol, CO_2. This is the chemical symbol for the carbon dioxide molecule, and means there are two oxygen atoms and one carbon atom.

See the little 2 after the O? The letters "di" in the word dioxide means two. Carbon dioxide (CO_2) is heavier than air (as we just demonstrated in the experiment), as it pushed the air up and out of the cup. CO_2 has no color or smell.

Carbon dioxide (CO_2) is used in fire extinguishers to put out some kinds of fires. It is also used in soda pop. When you open a bottle or can of soda pop, the fizz that comes out is carbon dioxide, or CO_2. Dry ice is made from frozen carbon dioxide.

13

Clues for case #2

1 Ziploc storage bag — quart size
2 paper cups — 3 oz. size
Baking soda — 2 heaping tbsp.
Vinegar — 1/2 cup

Begin your investigation

Take the Ziploc bag and practice opening and closing it (small children may need some help). In one of the paper cups measure in 2 heaping tbsp. of baking soda and in the other cup measure in 1/2 cup of vinegar. Take the cup with the baking soda in it and dump it into the Ziploc bag. Zip the bag 3/4 of the way, leaving just a small opening. Now, carefully pour the vinegar from the other cup into the Ziploc bag, quickly locking it. Make sure the Ziploc bag is tightly locked. Now shake or squeeze the bag gently to mix all of the contents. What is happening? What changes are you observing? Is the bag puffed up? How long will the Ziploc bag stay puffed up? What will happen if you open the Ziploc bag?

OUTSIDE GAS PRESSURE

Solution to Case #2

The bag is puffed up because of the gas being produced inside when we poured the vinegar into the baking soda. There is more gas pressure in the inside of the bag pushing at the walls of the bag than there is gas pressure on the outside walls of the bag.

SAFETY NOTE — Experiments that give off gas must never be performed in any closed container except a plastic bag. If you like, you may keep the bag closed and keep checking on it to see how long it will stay puffed up. Let's put our puffed up bags someplace where they won't be disturbed and see how long they stay puffed up.

Clues for case #3

1 glass bottle — 8 oz. size is good
1 plastic or metal funnel
1 balloon with the neck cut off
2 paper cups — 3 oz. size
Baking soda — 1 heaping tbsp.
Vinegar — 2 heaping tbsp.

Begin your investigation

Take the bottle and practice putting the balloon over the mouth of the bottle, being very careful not to tear the balloon. When you think you can do that easily, take the funnel and put it into the mouth of the bottle. Pour the baking soda into the bottle using the funnel. Now, quickly add the vinegar into the bottle through the funnel. Now hurry and lift off the funnel and quickly put the balloon over the mouth of the bottle. What is happening? What made the balloon get bigger? What is inside the balloon? What would have happened if the balloon weren't over the mouth of the bottle?

Solution to case #3

The carbon dioxide (CO_2) caused the balloon to expand. The balloon is full of carbon dioxide gas. The carbon dioxide gas would have gone into the air if the balloon weren't there to catch it.

How long do you think the balloon will stay blown up? Let's put the bottle with the balloon next to the puffed-up bag and see which one will last longer.

Clues for case #4 (case #4 should be done outside)
1 glass bottle — 8 oz. size is good
1 plastic or metal funnel
1 cork — to fit tightly into the small bottle
3 paper cups — 3 oz. size
Baking soda — 1 heaping tbsp.
Vinegar — 1/4 cup
Water 3 oz.

Begin your investigation

Pick up the cork and practice putting the cork in the bottle Make sure it fits nice and tight. Now take the cork and dip it into the cup with the water in it, wetting the cork. Put the funnel in the bottle and pour the baking soda through the funnel, into the bottle. Now do the same with the vinegar. Hurry and lift the funnel off the bottle and quickly put the cork into the bottle. Stand back. What happened to the cork? What made the cork pop out of the bottle?

Solution to case #4

The pressure inside the bottle, pushing up on the cork was greater than the pressure outside the bottle, pushing down on the cork. There were more molecules inside the bottle, pushing the cork up, than on the outside of the bottle.

17

The Mystery of the Silly Shapes

Your scientific mission for this experiment is to use your thinking powers and observation skills to explore and gather all the evidence you can. The secret code words are: properties, float and absorb. Good luck. This will now self-destruct in 1 minute. Gather these clues; you will need them to solve the following science cases.

Clues

1 pkg. Silly Putty
1 piece of clay
1 cup of water
1 plastic cup — 8 oz. or 10 oz. size
Large words cut from newspaper ads
1 rubber band

Gather these clues for case #1

1 pkg. Silly Putty
1 piece of clay

Begin your investigation

Take your Silly Putty out of the package (it comes in a plastic eggshell container) and smell it. Pick up the clay and compare it to the Silly Putty. Are they alike or different? Take the Silly Putty and mold it into different shapes. After each shape try bouncing the Silly Putty like a ball. What happened? Now rub the Silly Putty. What happens to the Silly Putty when you rub it? Now, take the Silly Putty and press it into your skin and then lift it off. What happened? Take the Silly Putty and stick it to a wall for a couple of minutes and lift it off. What happened? What properties have you discovered about Silly Putty from the investigations you have just completed?

Solution to case #1

Silly Putty smells good. Silly Putty is similar to clay, but they are different in many ways. If you drop Silly Putty like a ball, it will bounce, no matter what shape it is. When you rub it, it will get shiny. Silly Putty will pick up the patterns in your skin. If you stick Silly Putty on a wall, it will not leave a stain when you take it off the wall.

Gather these clues for case #2

1 pkg. Silly Putty
1 rubber band

Begin your investigation

Pick up the rubber band and stretch it back and forth several times. What happened when you stretched the rubber band? What happened when you stretched the Silly Putty? What differences did you discover? How are they alike?

Solution to case #2

Silly Putty stretches like a rubber band, but it will not go back to its original shape the way a rubber band will.

19

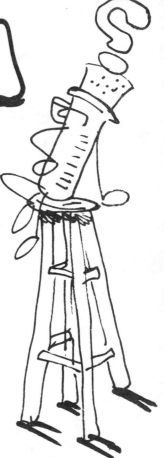

Gather these clues for case #3
1 pkg. Silly Putty
Large words cut from newspaper ads

Begin your investigation
Take the Silly Putty and press it onto words cut from the newspaper. Lift it off. Where did the letters go?

Solution to case #3
Silly Putty will pick up letters from the newspaper and make them appear backwards.

Gather these clues for case #4
1 pkg. Silly Putty
1 plastic cup — 8 oz. or 10 oz. (filled with cold tap water)

Begin your investigation
Take the Silly Putty and drop it into the water. Take the Silly Putty out of the water and feel it. What did you discover? Take the Silly Putty and mold it into different shapes. After each new shape put it into the water. Did the Silly Putty float after each new shape?

Solution to case #4
It is hard for Silly Putty to absorb water. Silly Putty floats only when it is the right shape.

The Case of the Appearing Colors

Your scientific mission for this experiment is to use your thinking powers and observation skills to explore and gather all the evidence you can. The secret code words are: rainbow, light, absorbed, reflected, refracted and spectrum. This next case can be investigated indoors or outdoors. Do it both ways. Good luck. This will now self-destruct in 1 minute. Gather these clues; you will need them to solve the following science case.

Clues
Bright sunshine
Hand mirror — any size
Tin foil pie plate
Water — enough to fill the pie plate
One piece of 8-1/2" x 11" unlined construction or regular paper

Begin your investigation

Take the pie plate and fill it with water. Put it on a table in a very bright, sunny room. Now place the mirror in the pan, so that the mirror is underwater and leaning against the side of the pan. Now position the pan so the sun is shining directly on the mirror. Move the mirror slowly in different directions, until you see a row of colors on the wall or ceiling. Do you see the colors on the wall or ceiling? Now let's try this investigation outside. Take all of your materials outside. Find a table in the sun. Fill up your pie plate with water and put it on the table. Now place the mirror in the pan so the mirror is underwater and leaning against the side of the pan. Now position the pan so the sun is shining directly on the mirror. Now take the piece of paper and put it in front of the pie plate and mirror and catch the colors on the paper. You might have to try different angles of the pie plate and mirror to get the sun to shine on the paper properly. Once you catch the colors on the paper, it is fun to count how many colors you see and how many different shapes or pictures you can make with the mirror by jiggling it. Did you make a rainbow? What did the rainbow look like? Where did all the beautiful colors come from? Can you name the colors you saw? What caused these colors to appear?

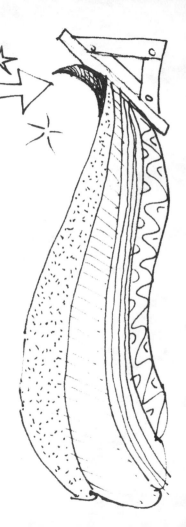

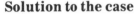

Solution to the case

When light strikes a solid object, it is absorbed or reflected. When light strikes a transparent object, such as a pan of water, light rays are bent or refracted. Different colors are bent at different angles, and when the light emerges, the colors will be broken apart into a rainbow effect.

As the sunlight hit the water, it slowed down, causing its colors to separate. Then the sunlight was reflected back from the mirror through the water and into the air, causing the colors to separate even further. That is why you could see them so clearly. This is how a rainbow is formed. Sunlight appears to be white, but it is really made up of red, orange, yellow, green, blue, indigo and violet. All these colors together are called the colors of the spectrum. Now, let's put away all of your supplies, being very careful not to break the mirror, because it is glass and could cut you if broken.

24

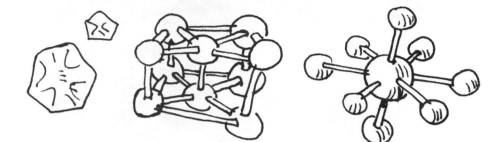

Mystery Concentrations

Your scientific mission for this experiment is to use your thinking powers and observation skills to explore and gather all the evidence you can. The secret code words are: solutions, concentrations, observations, substance, molecules, insoluble and soluble. Good luck. This will now self-destruct in 1 minute. Gather these clues; you will need them to solve the following science case.

Clues

Package of sugar sweetened Kool-Aid — any flavor
Straws
Measuring spoon — tsp. size
Measuring cup — 1/2 cup size
2 plastic cups — 8 or 10 oz. size, preferably ones that you can see through. Paper cups will work also.
Cold tap water

Begin your investigation

Take the 2 cups and in one of the cups measure in 2 tsp. of Kool-Aid and in the other cup measure 6 tsp. of Kool-Aid. Pick up the measuring cup and fill it with water. Pour 1/2 cup of water into each cup containing Kool-Aid. Now take the straw and taste the Kool-Aid in each cup. Tasting the Kool-Aid in this experiment is all right because it is a food, but other solutions should never be tasted unless you are told to do so by an adult and you are sure that the things you are tasting are absolutely safe. What are your observations from tasting and observing the Kool-Aid in each cup? Did we make a solution by mixing the Kool-Aid with the water? Why? How do the two Kool-Aid solutions differ in color and taste? Did we put the same amount of water into each cup of Kool-Aid powder? Did we put the same amount of Kool-Aid powder into each cup?

Solution to the case

Kool-Aid and water make a solution. When a solid substance (Kool-Aid) is mixed with a liquid (water), the solid seems to disappear, and goes into the solution. The molecules of the solid have spread among the molecules of the liquid. A substance that will not dissolve in liquid is called insoluble. A substance that will dissolve in liquid is called soluble. You probably observed that one cup of the Kool-Aid solution was lighter in color than the other one. When you tasted the Kool-Aid solution, you discovered that one cup tasted "watery" and that the other tasted "strong" or "delicious." The same amount of water was put into each cup, but the amount of the Kool-Aid powder was different in each cup. The reason the two solutions of Kool-Aid tasted and looked different was because they were different concentrations. The solution that tasted sweeter and looked darker in color is more concentrated than the watery solution. Please refer to the definition of concentration in the back of the book.

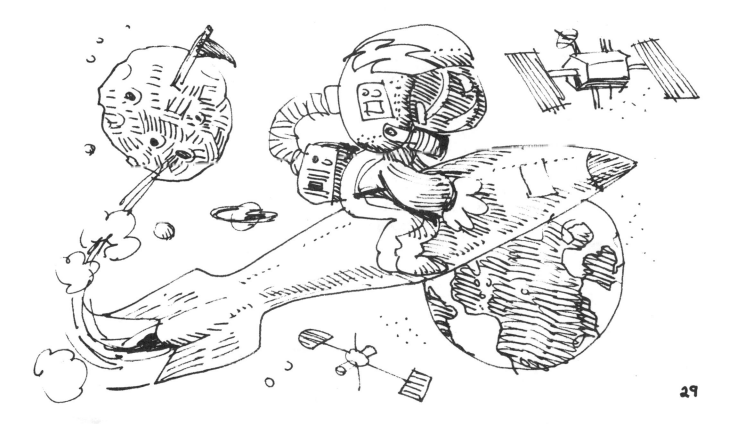

29

Mystery Lights

Your scientific mission for this experiment is to use your thinking powers and observation skills to explore and gather all the evidence you can. The secret code words are: light bulb, voltage (volts), battery, filament, contact, conductor, positive, negative, electricity, circuit, and vacuum. Good luck. This will now self-destruct in 1 minute. Gather these clues; you will need them to solve the following science cases.

Clues
Light bulb #222 (called lamps)—
Radio Shack has this size
2 batteries — size D 1.5 volts
Tin foil — 12 inches long by 5 inches wide
Hand magnifier
Scotch tape

Gather these clues for case #1
1 lamp #222
Tin foil — 12 inches by 5 inches
Hand magnifier
1 battery — size D 1.5 volt

Begin your investigation

Pick up the battery and examine it well. The battery has a top and a bottom. The positive (+) end is the end of the battery with the bump. The negative (−) end is the end of the battery that is flat. The top and bottom of the battery are made of steel. The sides are made of cardboard, which may also be covered with metal. The side of the battery with the letter on it tells you the size you have. The numbers with V after them tells you how many volts it has. Your batteries are size D and have 1.5 volts. Now, pick up the lamp, being very careful with it, because it is made of thin glass and will break if dropped and could cut you if broken. Pick up the hand magnifier and look closely at the inside of the lamp. You will see a small wire that looks like a spring. This is called the filament. The filament is connected to the larger conductor wires. The two large wires do not touch each other. The large wires are attached in the base of the lamp. At the bottom of the bulb is a metal button, called a contact. The side of the lamp is also a contact. Now, let's make the lamp light up. Take the piece of tin foil and fold it the long way again and again and again and again, until you have a thin strip. Take your lamp, battery and thin strip of tin foil and try to make your lamp light. Experiment with different ways to get you light to go on. If you can't figure out how to turn on the lamp after a short while, I will tell you how.

GOOD IDEA

Place the battery, negative end down, on top of the tin foil and take the light bulb and hold it on top of the battery (positive end). With your hand bring the end of the strip of foil and press it against the base (conductor) of the bulb and the lamp will light. Why did the light go on?

Solution to case #1

Electricity travels through materials called conductors. Metals are good conductors. Non-metals are poor conductors. To create electricity you must have a complete circuit or path to make lamps light and motors turn. If the circuit is not complete, electricity will not flow. The circuit must lead from one end of the battery to the bulb. This then goes through the filament. It is the filament in the electric lamp that gets white hot because electricity is going through it. It does not burn up because there is no oxygen in the lamp. You cannot have fire without oxygen. In the lamp there is a vacuum or gas that will not support fire. It then goes back to the other end of the battery.

Clues for case #2

1 lamp #222
2 batteries — size D 1.5 volts
Tin foil — 12 inches by 5 inches
Scotch tape

Begin your investigation

How can we make the light brighter? Pick up the two batteries and tape them together. The negative end of one battery must connect or be against the positive end of the other battery. Now place the bulb and tin foil the same as you did in case #1. Is the light brighter? Why?

Solution to case #2

Your light is brighter because you have more voltage. (1.5 volts in one battery, 1.5 volts in the other battery.) 1.5 volts plus 1.5 volts equals 3 volts. You have twice as much electricity. However, if the light bulb is rated 1.5 volts, it will burn out at this higher voltage.

Mystery Attractions

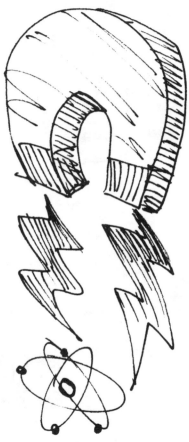

Your scientific mission for this experiment is to use your thinking powers and observation skills to explore and gather all the evidence you can. The secret code words are magnets, object, and polarity. Good luck. This will now self-destruct in 1 minute. Gather these clues; you will need them to solve the following science cases.

Clues

1 shoebox
1 magnet in the shape of a bar, U or horseshoe
1 disk magnet (available at Radio Shack or other electronics or hardware store)
1 handkerchief or a square piece of cloth
Lots of paper clips and steel nails (short and long)
Steel or iron pins
Plastic buttons
Copper pennies
Rocks
1 small square piece of paper
1 plastic glass or cup — 8 oz. or 10 oz. size
1 piece of string about 10 inches long
1 plastic lid from any coffee can
Water — ¾ cup

Gather these clues for case #1
6 paper clips
1 shoebox
6 pins
6 small nails
3 buttons
3 pennies
3 rocks
1 disk magnet

Begin your investigation

Put all the items except the magnet in a box. Now mix them all up. With the magnet, separate all the contents of the box into groups according to likeness.

Did you find the magnet could easily pick up and separate pins, small nails and paper clips? Did you find that the magnet could not pick up the buttons or the pennies?

Do you know why the magnet could pick up some of the objects but not pick up all the objects?

Solution to case #1

Objects like paper clips, nails and pins are made of iron or steel and are drawn to a magnet. Objects such as buttons and pennies are made of plastic and copper and are not drawn to the magnet.

Gather these clues for case #2

1 disk magnet
1 piece of string about 10 inches long
1 plastic glass or cup 8 oz. or 10 oz. size
Water — ¾ cup
5 paper clips

Begin your investigation

Place 5 paper clips in your cup. Fill your cup with the water. Tie a piece of string to the disk magnet. Now take the magnet and using it like a fishing pole, go fishing and see if the magnet will catch any paper clips. Are you catching any paper clips? Why?

Solution to case #2

Magnets can act through water.

MAGNETIC

Gather these clues for case #3
1 disk magnet or horseshoe magnet
1 plastic glass or cup — 8 oz. or 10 oz.
6 paper clips
Begin your investigation
Put the paper clips into the cup. Using the magnet only on the **outside** of the cup, can you lift the paper clips out of the cup? Why?

Solution to case #3
Magnets can act through glass.

Gather these clues for case #4
1 handkerchief or piece of cloth
10 paper clips
1 magnet — horseshoe, U-shaped or disk shaped
Begin your investigation
Take the handkerchief or piece of cloth, and wrap it around the magnet. Put the paper clips on a table. Try to pick up the paper clips with your covered magnet. Did they come up? Why?

Solution to case #4
Magnets can act through cloth.

Gather these clues for case #5
1 disk magnet
1 plastic lid from a coffee can
10 paper clips
Begin your investigation
  Put the paper clips into the plastic lid. Now take the magnet and slide it under the lid. What is happening? Why?
  Keep sliding it under the lid and with a little practice you can create some very unusual designs.
Solution to case #5
  Magnets can act through plastic.

Gather these clues for case #6
1 bar magnet
10 paper clips
Begin your investigation
  Put the paper clips on a table in a row or circle. Take the bar magnet and try to pick up the paper clips one at a time without touching the magnet to the paper clips. Can this be done? Why?
Solution to case #6
  Magnets can act through air.

Gather these clues for case #7
1 bar magnet
1 long nail
1 piece of paper
Begin your investigation
  Take the nail and put it on a table. Put a piece of paper over the nail. Take the bar magnet and try to pick up the nail through the paper. Did the magnet pick up the nail? Why?
Solution to case #7
  Magnets can act through paper.

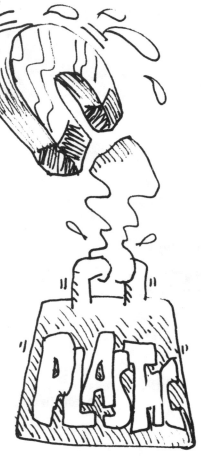

38

Gather these clues for case #8

1 bar magnet
10 paper clips
10 nails

Begin your investigation

Put the nails and the paper clips in a pile on a table. Take the bar magnet and try to pick up the paper clips and nails with the different parts of the magnet. Which part of the magnet did you pick up the most paper clips with? Why?

Solution to case #8

A magnet has its strongest attraction at its ends. These are known as the north and south poles of the magnet. That is, magnets have polarity. The horseshoe or U-shaped magnet is made from a bar that is bent so that the poles or strongest parts are close together. This increases the strength of the magnet and it can lift more.

What happens if you put two horseshoe magnets with the north pole of one opposite the north pole of the other. Are they attracting each other? No, they are repelling one another; like poles repel and opposites attract.

Some magnetic materials occur in nature, but most are manufactured by using large charges of electricity in certain materials. Some magnets are permanent and some are not.

If you are interested in magnetism, go to your library. There are lots of books there on this subject.

Mystery of Water and Ice

Your scientific mission for this experiment is to use your thinking powers and observation skills to explore and gather all the evidence you can. The secret code words are ice cubes, water vapor, air, condense, humidity, and moisture.

Good luck. This will now self-destruct in 1 minute. Gather these clues; you will need them to solve the following science cases.

Clues

Lots of ice — large size pieces

Ice chest — to keep ice from melting

Empty small tin cans — 5 oz. shiny on outside of can (the cans that the snack pack pudding comes in is a perfect size for this experiment)

Water — cold from tap

Food coloring (any color you have on hand)

A hand magnifying glass

Paper cups — 10 oz. and 8 oz. sizes

Plastic spoons

Salt — loose in shakers

Measuring cup

String — a piece 10-12 inches long

Gather these clues for case #1

3 empty tin cans (the kind snack pack pudding comes in)

Ice chest — to keep ice from melting

6 ice cubes

1 paper cup (10 oz. size)

Water — cold from tap

1 plastic spoon

¼ cup of salt

A hand magnifying glass

Begin your investigation

Take the paper cup and put about 2 drops of food coloring in it and fill the cup with water. Put 2 ice cubes in each of the tin cans (making sure that the shiny part on the outside of the can is dry). Set aside one of the tin cans with the ice in it, and into the second tin can, pour water from your cup, filling it almost to the top. Now set aside that cup. Pour the rest of the water into tin can #3, and start adding the salt, a little at a time, stirring with your spoon after each addition. After all the salt has been added, observe what is happening. What is happening to the outside of tin can #3?

Take your hand magnifier and look closely at the outside of the tin cans. In 10 to 20 minutes, you will see something happen. Water is forming on the outside of the can. Where did the water droplets that are on the outside of the 3 tin cans come from? Why isn't the water on the outside of the cans colored like the colored water inside the cans? When you looked at the water droplets through the hand magnifier, were the droplets easier to see?

41

Solution to case #1

The water droplets on the outside of the can with only the ice in it were formed because the ice in the can cooled the sides, and the warmer air on the outside of the can that came in contact with the tin can was cooled.

The water droplets on the outside of the can with the ice and water in it formed because the ice in the can cooled the water, and the water cooled the sides of the can and the air on the outside of the can that came in contact with the tin can was cooled.

The water droplets on the outside of the can with the ice water and salt in it formed droplets on the outside because the ice cooled the water, and the water cooled the sides. The salt helped to melt the ice more quickly which condensed the moisture in the air more quickly.

The water vapor in the air changed into (condensed) water, collecting as water droplets on the outside of the cup. The amount of moisture or water in the air is called humidity. It is safe to taste the water droplets as they are pure water removed from the air.

Now you know why the water on the outside of the tin can is not colored like the colored water inside the tin can. Remember, the water on the outside of the can is not the same water as on the inside of the can.

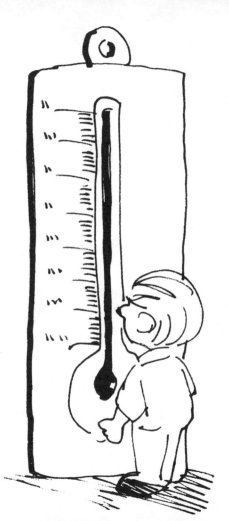

Gather these clues for case #2

1 tin can (the kind snack pack pudding comes in)

Ice chest — to keep ice from melting

1 piece of string 10-12 inches long

1 salt shaker

1 paper cup (5 oz.) — filled with cold water from tap

1 or 2 large ice cubes

Begin your investigation

Pour the water from the paper cup into the can, filling it to the top. Now take the piece of string and dip it into the water and wet it completely. After the string is wet, put it down next to the tin can. Take 1 or 2 ice cubes and put them into the tin can (making sure the ice is floating as near to the top as you can get it to). Now carefully lay the string over the ice cube (now the string should be touching the ice cube) with the ends of the string hanging down each side of the glass. Pick up the salt shaker and sprinkle a little salt onto the part of the string that is touching the ice cube, and count to 60. Now carefully pull up on both ends of the string and you should be able to lift the ice cube from the can of water with just the string. If this doesn't work the first time, add more salt and count to 70 and try again. Did you just lift an ice cube out of the can of water with just a thin piece of string. Is string that strong? How did you get the string to stick to the ice cube?

Solution to case #2

The salt melted the ice, then the ice froze the string, freezing the string firmly inside the ice cube.

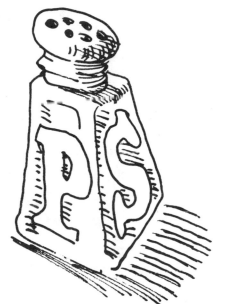

Mystery of Growth

Your scientific mission for this experiment is to use your thinking powers and observation skills to explore and gather all the evidence you can. The secret code words are soil, seeds, temperature, moisture, and oxygen. Good luck. This will now self-destruct in 1 minute. Gather these clues; you will need them to solve the following case.

Clues

3 planter pots — clear plastic with drainage holes
1 bag of potting soil
3 large Ziploc bags
1 plastic bag
12 sunflower seeds

½ cup of water
Marking pen
Old newspapers
3 stick-on labels

Preparation for the investigation

A few days before you begin this investigation, take one of the planting pots and fill the pot up to the top with potting soil. Now dump that on a piece of newspaper and put it in the sun or under a lamp until it is completely dry (it takes a few days to completely dry out the soil). When the soil is completely dry, put the soil in an unsealed plastic bag and mark the bag "dry soil."

Begin your investigation

Gather all the clues for this case and have them handy for use. Take the three labels and with a marking pen, write "dry soil" on one label, write "moist soil" on another label, and "wet soil" on the last label. Stick one label on each of the Ziploc bags. Pick up one of the pots and put some of the dry soil you prepared a few days ago in it, filling the pot ¾ of the way. Now take 4 sun-flower seeds and gently push these into the dry soil in the pot. Now sprinkle a little more dry soil on top. Put this pot in the Ziploc bag labeled "dry soil" and close the bag tightly.

Take another pot and fill the pot ¾ of the way with potting soil you bought at the store. Take 4 sunflower seeds and push these gently into the soil, then sprinkle a little soil on top. Put this pot in the Ziploc bag labeled "moist soil" and close the bag tightly.

Take the third pot and fill it ¾ of the way with the soil you bought from the store. Take ½ cup of water and mix the water into the soil making it wet. Take 4 sunflower seeds and gently push them into the soil. Then sprinkle a little wet soil on top. Put this pot in the Ziploc bag labeled "wet soil."

Take the three bags with the plants in them and carefully (holding the bottoms of the pots in the bags) put them in a place that is **not** near a heater or in direct sunlight. A counter near a window is best.

These plants should be left alone for one week and not watered during that week. You should check on them during the week. When checking on the plants during the week, open each Ziploc bag and look inside and observe what is happening. After you have checked on the plants, make sure that you reseal the bags tightly.

Which seeds do you think will grow the best in one week? Why do you think that?

What do seeds need in order to grow?

After one week, what happened to the seeds in the three pots with different moisture levels?

Solution to the case

Seeds in order to grow need soil, water, air, light and the proper temperature. All these conditions affect the growth of seeds.

After one week, you will find that the seeds in the dry soil did not grow. The seeds in the moist soil have begun to grow into plants. Your Ziploc bags have created a "green house" effect and have trapped the moisture from the soil and kept it in the atmosphere of the plants. You can actually feel the moisture on the inside of the bag with your hand. The plant in the wet soil will probably show the most growth. After one week, the sunflower seeds should have both roots and stems.

Environment plays a big part in the proper growth of seeds. Several factors are important for this growth to take place. They are proper temperature, sufficient moisture, and sufficient carbon dioxide. Plants do not require oxygen to grow. Plants produce or give off oxygen through photosynthesis.

Mystery Bubbles

Your scientific mission for this experiment is to use your thinking powers and observation skills to explore and gather all the evidence you can. The secret code words are light, tube, surface, soap film, component, object, and pattern. The next case should be investigated outdoors. Good luck. This will now self-destruct in 1 minute. Gather these clues; you will need them to solve the following science cases.

Clues

Liquid dishwashing soap — use Joy or Ajax brands

Measuring spoon — tbsp.
Water — cold from tap (one quart)
Lots of empty containers or cans of different diameters and some the same size that you can make into tubes by removing both ends
2 plastic straws
String 2 to 3 feet long
1 roll of black electrical tape — you can get this at most supermarkets and large drug stores
Pan — plastic or metal, 2 or 3 inches deep to hold the soap solution
1 plastic bowl of cold water from tap
1 roll of paper towels

Gather these clues for case #1

Dishwashing liquid — Joy or Ajax
Measuring spoon — tbsp.
Lots of empty containers made into tubes
Water — cold from tap
Pan — plastic or metal

Begin your investigation

Measure 8 tbsp. of the dishwashing liquid and put into pan. Add one quart of water to the pan and mix the soap with the water. Pick up a tube that you made by removing both ends of a container or can. Take the tube and stick one end of it into the soap solution leaving it there for about 20 seconds. After you get a good soap "window" across one end, pull it out carefully and blow gently through the other open end without the soap film on it. When you see the bubble forming, slowly twist the tube a little bit in one direction and this will free the bubble into the air. Did your bubble get very big? Did the bubbles break right away when they went into the air? Did you try popping the bubbles with your hands? Were your hands wet or dry when you tried to pop the bubbles? Did the bubbles pop?

Solution to case #1

The size of your bubbles will depend a lot on the size of the container you used to blow them. A large coffee can (3 lb. size) will make larger bubbles than a small orange juice can. You can use any objects found around the house for blowing bubbles as long as there is an opening where a soap film can be formed. Did you notice that some bubbles broke quicker than others? Lots of factors cause this to happen. The soap film can break if the force of the rushing air was too great, or the wind can cause a bubble to break. Also, if the container wasn't left in the soap solution long enough to form a good soap "window" the bubble may break. And if it was left in too long, it may break. If you tried to break the bubble with your hand, you probably discovered these things happening:

If your hands were dry, the bubble broke immediately. When dry objects touch wet objects the surface of the wet object is broken. If your hands were wet, the bubble will not break as rapidly.

Gather these clues for case #2

Dishwashing soap solution (as in case #1)

Pan — plastic or metal

Lots of empty tubes

1 roll of black electrician tape

Begin your investigation

Make the soap solution using 8 tbsp. of soap to 1 quart of water. Now take a few tubes (2, 3, 4, or more) and tape them together at one of the opened ends. Dip one of the opened ends into the soap

50

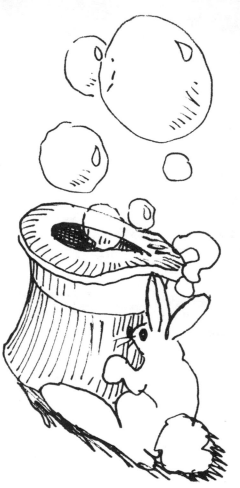

solution, leaving it there for 10 to 20 seconds or until a soap "window" forms on the end of the tubes. Lift it out of the soap solution and blow gently but with enough force so a bubble forms at the end of the tube. Now carefully twist the can a little so the bubble will float away from the tube going into the air. Are these bubbles bigger than in case #1? Are the bubbles lasting longer once up in the air than in case #1? Why is this happening?

Solution to case #2

When you use more than one tube to blow bubbles, you will discover that the other end of the tube will be farther from your mouth, and the flow of air through it will be smoother. These bubbles will not break away as easily as the ones blown from just one tube. The wider the tube, the bigger the bubbles.

Helpful Hint:
Use 2/3 cup Joy or Dawn and 2 Tbsp. of liquid glycerin (optional) to 14 cups water. Let stand overnight for best results.

Gather these clues for case #3
2 plastic straws
String — 2 to 4 feet long
Dishwashing soap solution
Pan — plastic or metal
1 plastic bowl of cold water from the tap
1 roll of paper towels

Begin your investigation
Pick up the string and thread it through both straws, tying the two ends together in a small knot. You have now made a frame. Place the frame into the pan of soap solution and leave it there for about 10 to 20 seconds, carefully lifting it out after you have a soap-film "window" stretched across the frame. Your hands will get soapy as you do this. The soapier your hands and straws are, the bigger the bubble will be, and the longer it will last.

Caution: Be very careful not to touch your face while doing this experiment. When your hands get too soapy you can wash them in the bowl of water and dry them with a paper towel. After you wash your hands, put fresh water into the clean water bowl so it is clean for the next time.

After the soap film is stretched across the frame, hold the frame out in front of you just below your waist, and carefully pull the frame upward. As the frame is moving upward, a bubble will form. After the bubble forms, gently bring the two straws together and step back. The bubble will separate from the frame. You will have to practice this and have some patience. Eventually, you will see huge, gigantic bubbles floating up and away. As these large bubbles are floating in the air, do you see colors in them? How many different colors do you see? Did you see your face in the frame when you were making the soap "window"? Do you see different patterns in the bubbles?

Solution to case #3

You will see many different colors and the colors will change depending at which angle the sun is hitting the bubble. Also you will see different patterns in the bubbles. The different colors you see are the colors of the spectrum. They are caused by sunlight being broken up into its component colors as the light is slowed by the bubble. Do you remember this from the mirror and pan of the water experiment you did earlier in this book?

You can see your face in the soap "window" as it is in a mirror.

Absorb— to suck up or drink.

Air— a mixture of gases, made up mainly of oxygen, hydrogen and nitrogen atoms.

Atom— a tiny body composed of a nucleus with a cloud of electron particles circulating around it. It is the smallest basic unit of matter to make an element. It is less than a billionth of an inch in diameter. Everything in the world is made up of atoms. Atoms combine to form molecules.

Average— a numerical result obtained by dividing the sum of two or more numbers by the amount of numbers. Example: $1+2+3=6 \div 3=2$.

Battery— a cell storing an electrical charge and capable of furnishing a current.

Chemical change— involves changing a substance into another kind of substance.

Circuit— the path electricity travels from one terminal of a battery to the other.

CO₂— the chemical symbol for the carbon dioxide molecule. There are two oxygen atoms and one carbon atom.

Component— a part, a constituent, an ingredient.

Compute— to number, to count, to ascertain, to determine.

Concentration— the strength or density of a solution.

Condense— when water vapor cools, it may condense as water droplets. It becomes reduced to a denser form; there are more atoms in a given volume.

Conductor— a substance, commonly a metal such as copper or aluminum, through which electricity will flow.

Contact— a device for making an electrical connection.

Dissolving— to appear to disappear into a liquid or a melting.

Electricity— a form of energy which has the electron as its fundamental unit.

Evaporation— the process of a liquid changing into a gas, or to change from a solid or a liquid into a gas.

Expand— to take up more space, to increase size.

Filament— a thin wire inside an electric bulb that glows white hot and gived off light when an electric current passes through it.

Float— to rest on the surface of a liquid.

Gas— a material that has no definite shape or volume but which expands to take the shape of its container.

H_2O— the chemical symbol for water. H_2 means that every molecule of water has 2 atoms of hydrogen. O means that every molecule of water has one atom of oxygen.

Humidity— the invisible water vapor which is present in the air.

Ice cubes— frozen water.

Insoluble— a substance that will not dissolve in a liquid.

Invisible— not visible; that cannot be seen.

Lamp— any device for producing light.

Light— the bright form of energy given off by something that enables one to see.

Magnet— iron or steel that has the property to attract other iron or steel.

Maximum— the greatest amount.

Minimum— the lowest amount.

Moisture— water or other liquid causing a slight wetness or dampness.

Molecule— the smallest part of an element or compound that has the properties of the substance.

Negative— having more electrons than protons.

Object— something that may be seen or felt.

Observations— the gathering of information by seeing or noting facts.

Oxygen— a chemical element found in the air as a colorless, odorless, tasteless gas that is essential to life and is involved in the burning process.

Pattern— to make or design.

Physical change— any change in matter that does not change its chemical composition.

Polarity— relating to a pole of a magnet.

Positive— having a deficiency of electrons, being a part from which the electric current flows to the external circuit.

Pressure— exerting force over a surface.

Property— a special quality or characteristic of a thing.

Range— to vary within limits.

Rainbow— a spectrum formed by the reflection and refraction of light at the surface of small droplets of water in the air.

Reaction— a change that occurs as a result of mixing two or more materials together.

Reflect— to be bent or thrown back.

Refract— to bend (a ray of light) as it passes from one medium into another.

Seed— a miniature dormant plant in a protective coating and often with its own food supply that is capable of developing under suitable conditions into a plant.

Soap film— a thin membrane of soap.

Soluble— the ability of a substance to dissolve in another substance; a substance that will dissolve in liquid.

Solutions— a mixture of two substances, one of which is dissolved in the other. This results when a substance dissolves in a liquid.

Spectrum— the colors in a thin beam of mixed light, separated and arranged side by side in order of increasing wave length.

Steam— water vapor at or above its boiling temperature.

Substance— the physical matter of which a thing consists.

Surface— the outside or exterior of an object.

Surface area— the outside of an object that is exposed.

Temperature— the degree of hotness or coldness. Temperature is measured by a thermometer.

Tube— a hollow elongated cylinder.

Vacuum— a space which is empty of all matter including air.

Visible— that which can be seen.

Voltage— a measure of the electrical pressure in a circuit.

Water vapor— water that has changed from a liquid to a gas.

Get Your Official Backyard Scientist Certificate and Join the Backyard Scientist Club!

Just print your name and address on a slip of paper and state that you have completed all the experiments in the book. Include 55 cents in stamps and I will send you your official Backyard Scientist Certificate and enroll you in the Backyard Scientist Club. Also, The Backyard Scientist would like to know which experiments you liked best and why.

Write to: Backyard Scientist
P.O. Box 16966
Irvine, CA 92623

Lab Notes

Lab Notes

Lab Notes

Lab Notes